Christopher Rouse
Heimdall's Trumpet

for Solo Trumpet and Orchestra
(Piano Reduction)

HENDON MUSIC

BOOSEY & HAWKES

AN IMAGEM COMPANY

DISTRIBUTED BY

HAL•LEONARD®
CORPORATION
7777 W. BLUEMOUND RD. P.O. BOX 13819 MILWAUKEE, WI 53213

www.boosey.com
www.halleonard.com

Published by Hendon Music, Inc.
a Boosey & Hawkes company
229 West 28th Street, 11th Fl.
New York NY 10001

www.boosey.com

© Copyright 2012 by Hendon Music Inc.
a Boosey & Hawkes company
Copyright for all countries. All rights reserved.

ISMN 979-0-051-10753-7

First printed 2013

Printed and distributed by Hal Leonard Corporation, Milwaukee WI

Commissioned for the Chicago Symphony Orchestra, Riccardo Muti, Music Director, by the Edward F. Schmidt Family Commissioning Fund. Premiered on December 20, 2012 by the Chicago Symphony Orchestra, Jaap van Zweden conductor, Christopher Martin trumpet soloist

Written for the Chicago Symphony Orchestra for its principal trumpeter, Christopher Martin, *Heimdall's Trumpet* was completed in Baltimore, Maryland on January 21, 2012. The title of the work refers to the Nordic god Heimdall, whose blasts on his trumpet to announce the onset of Ragnarok, the Norse equivalent of Armageddon.

Cast in four movements, the title *Heimdall's Trumpet* refers properly to the finale, which attempts in a general way to depict these mythological events as I imagine them. The onset of Ragnarok occurs only at the very end of the work, in a very short orchestral fortissimo outburst followed by an extended silence. The first movement is declamatory in nature and gives way to a whirlwind scherzo that utilizes a variety of mutes for both the soloist and the orchestral brass section. The third movement is a largo that swings like a pendulum between sections of substantive dissonance and straightforward consonance. The aforementioned finale, more specifically dramatic and programmatic in nature, returns to the more aggressive world of the first movement.

The solo trumpet part requires much of the player, who must possess enormous technical prowess, including the ability to produce pedal tones at some length.

Heimdall's Trumpet calls for an orchestra consisting of three flutes (third doubling piccolo), three oboes, three clarinets, three bassoons (third doubling contrabassoon), four horns, three trumpets, three trombones, tuba, harp, timpani, percussion (three players), and strings. It lasts approximately twenty-two minutes.

— Christopher Rouse

INSTRUMENTATION

3 Flutes (3rd doubling on Piccolo)

3 Oboes

3 B♭ Clarinets

3 Bassoons (3rd doubling on Contrabassoon)

4 F Horns

3 C Trumpets

3 Trombones

Tuba

Timpani

3 Percussion

(chinese cymbal, xylophone, anvil, 2 snare drums,
cymbals, hammer, tenor drum, tam-tam,
glockenspiel, suspended cymbal, metal plate,
bass drum, chimes, field drum, bongos, gong)

Harp

Solo Trumpet in C

Strings

Duration: ca. 22 minutes

to Christopher Martin

HEIMDALL'S TRUMPET

I.

Piano reduction by Chitose Okashiro

CHRISTOPHER ROUSE

979-0-051-10753-7

This reduction is intended for rehearsal purposes and not for performance use.

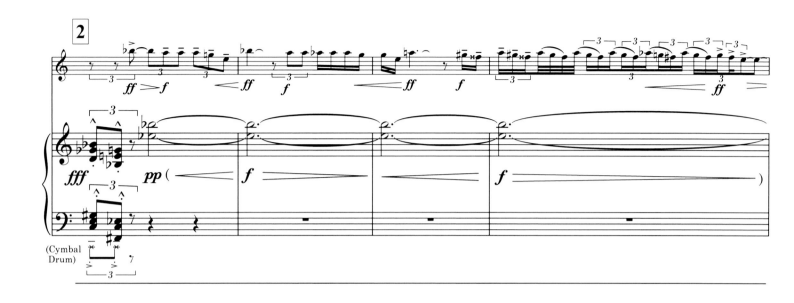

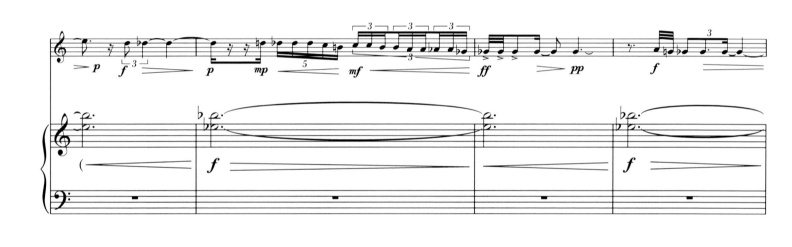

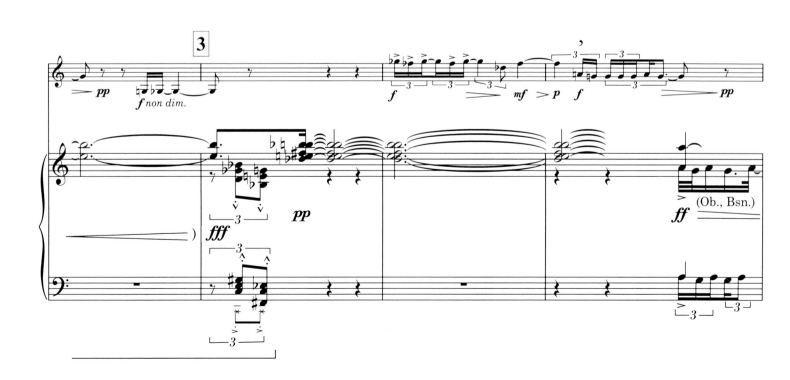

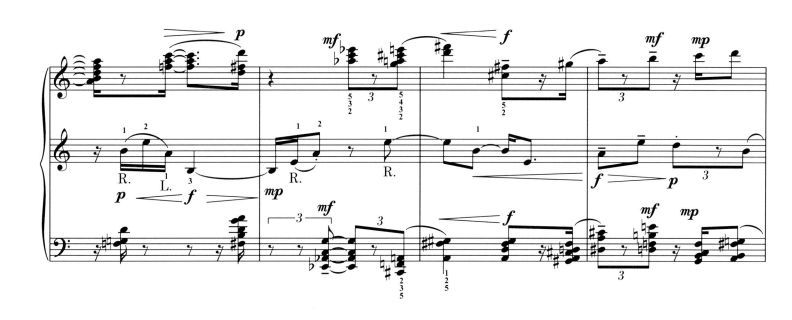

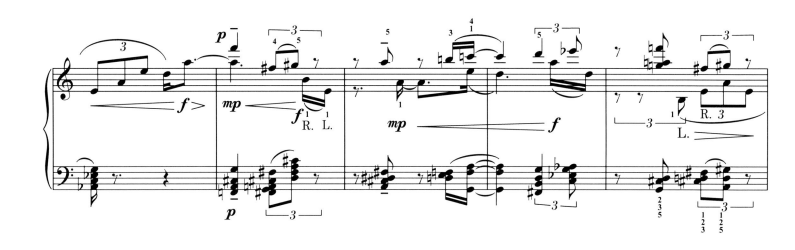

attacca

II.

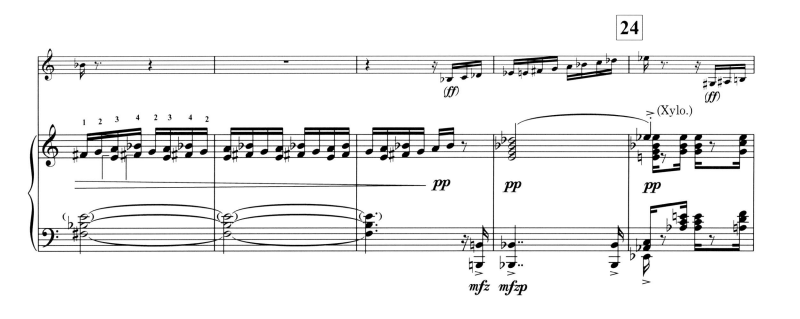

Christopher Rouse
Heimdall's Trumpet

for Solo Trumpet and Orchestra
(Piano Reduction)

HENDON MUSIC

BOOSEY & HAWKES

AN IMAGEM COMPANY

DISTRIBUTED BY

HAL•LEONARD®
CORPORATION
7777 W. BLUEMOUND RD. P.O. BOX 13819 MILWAUKEE, WI 53213

www.boosey.com
www.halleonard.com

INSTRUMENTATION

3 Flutes (3rd doubling on Piccolo)

3 Oboes

3 B♭ Clarinets

3 Bassoons (3rd doubling on Contrabassoon)

4 F Horns

3 C Trumpets

3 Trombones

Tuba

Timpani

3 Percussion

(chinese cymbal, xylophone, anvil, 2 snare drums,
cymbals, hammer, tenor drum, tam-tam,
glockenspiel, suspended cymbal, metal plate,
bass drum, chimes, field drum, bongos, gong)

Harp

Solo Trumpet in C

Strings

Duration: ca. 22 minutes

HEIMDALL'S TRUMPET

I.

CHRISTOPHER ROUSE

SOLO TRUMPET in C

2

4

attacca

III.

10

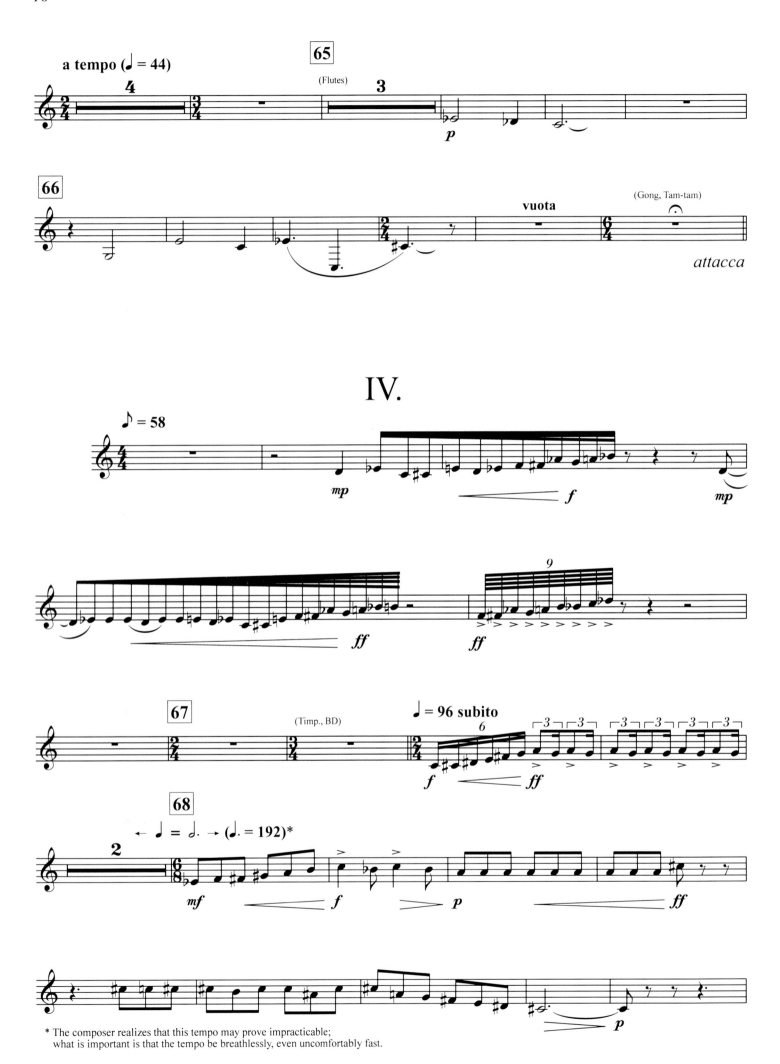

IV.

* The composer realizes that this tempo may prove impracticable;
  what is important is that the tempo be breathlessly, even uncomfortably fast.

12

14

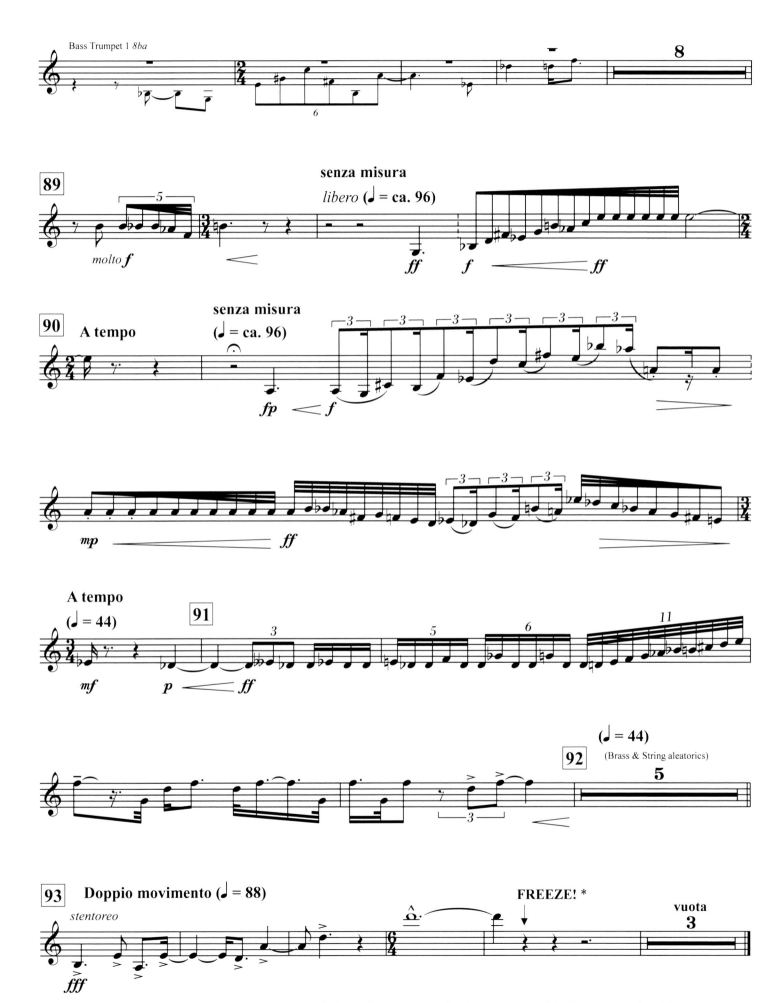

attacca

III.

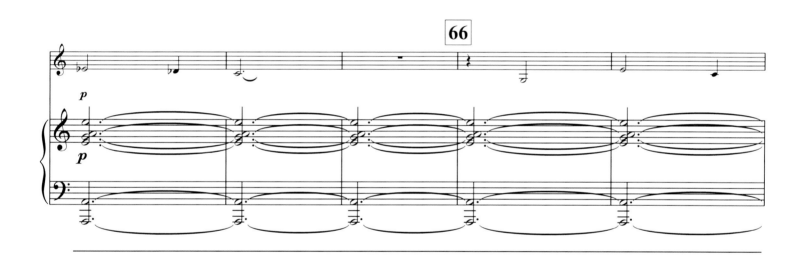

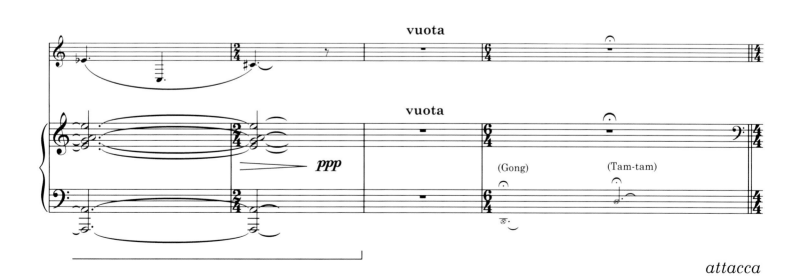

attacca

IV.

* The composer realizes that this tempo may prove impracticable; what is important is that the tempo be breathlessly, even uncomfortably fast.

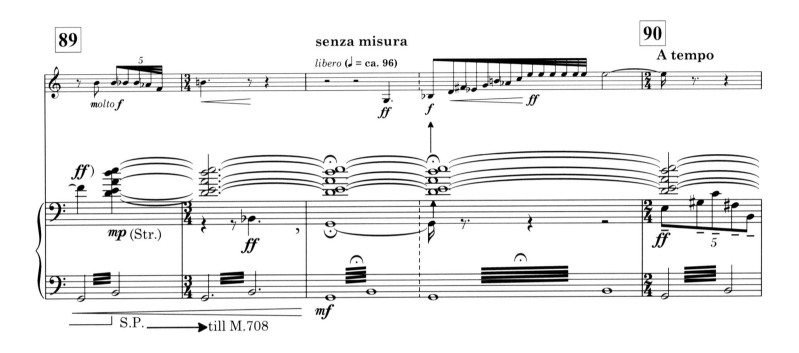

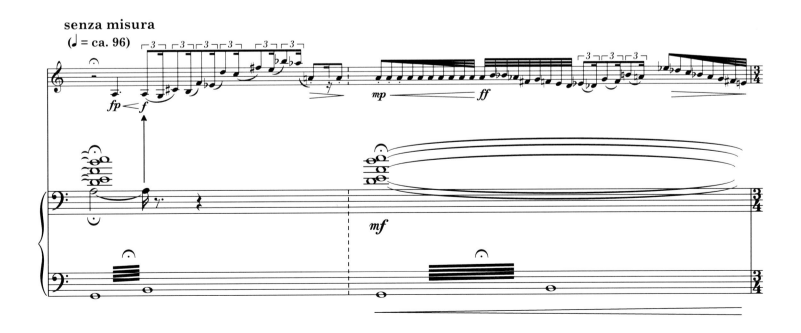

The conductor and all performers should remain absolutely motionless
while the conductor silently counts the remaining beats to him or herself.

FREEZE!

Hammer, Tam-tam, BD

Deo Gratias
January 21, 2012
Baltimore, Maryland